How do you like our book?

We would really appreciate you leaving

GW00420612

Other Picture Books:

For other fun Picture Books by Kampelstone,
simply search for:

Kampelstone Picture Books

FACTS ABOUT RUSSIA

- Russia is the largest country in the world by area. Its total land area is 6,599,921 square miles (17,098,242 square kilometers).

- The land border of Russia is 20,241 kilometers long, the second longest of any country.

- The Trans-Siberian Railway spans almost all the way across the county, making it the single longest passenger railway in the world. It covers 5700 miles (9200 kilometers) going between Moscow, into Asia and ending at Vladivostok on the fat eastern edge of Russia on the Sea of Japan. There is a longer railway (8100 miles – 13000 km) running between Yiwu, just south of Shanghai, and traveling all the way to Madrid, Spain, but this is a freight train only.

- Russia shares a border with 14 countries including Norway, Finland, Estonia, Latvia, Lithuania, Poland, Belarus, China, Ukraine, Georgia, Azerbaijan, Kazakhstan, Mongolia and North Korea. No other country in the world has as many borders.

- There are nine time zones across Russia. Russia is permanently on daylight savings time.

- Moscow's metro system is the fastest means of transport. During rush hour, trains arrive every 90 seconds. More than 9 million passengers ride the Metro every day.

- Russia is the third largest producer of oil in the world, after Saudi Arabia and the United States.

- Russian's never shake hands in a doorway. They believe it is bad luck will lead to an argument.

- Russia has 12 active volcanoes.

- Lake Baikal contains 22% of the world's fresh water and is the deepest lake as well as the oldest freshwater lake in the world. It is 25 to 30 million years old. It contains 1,700 species of plants and animals, two thirds of which are unique to the lake.

- The Volga river is the longest in Russia at 2190 miles (3,530 kilometers) long. Its source is in the Valdai Hills northwest of Moscow and runs all the way to the Caspian Sea.

- More than half of Russia is covered in forest land.

- Life expectancy in Russia for males is 67 years and 77 years for females.

- There are some 10 million more women in Russia than there are men.

- A man will never give an even number of flowers to a woman. It is considered bad luck and is associated with funerals.

- Russia's high literacy rate is very high at 99.7% of the population able to read and write by the age of fifteen.

- Russian is the seventh most spoken language in the world with 258 million speakers.

- Russians use the Cyrillic alphabet instead of the Latin alphabet. The Cyrillic alphabet originated in Bulgaria and is based on the Greek alphabet.

- Russia and the United States are actually quite close to one another geographically. Big Diomede Island, Russia, in the Bering Strait, is 2.4 miles (3.9 km) from the United States island Diomede Island, Alaska.

- The larch tree is the most common tree in Russia. And it's an amazing fact that 25% of the world's standing forest is in Russia.

- The most famous animal in Russia is the Siberian tiger. They are rare and an endangered species.

- Russia has a national sex day, known as Procreation Day. It takes place each year on the 12th of September. Its purpose is for Russians to take a day off in order to make babies and it seems to be working. Every June, there is an increase in births and the rates are higher than any other month. Couples who give birth nine months later on Russia's national day, the 12th of June, receive money, cars, refrigerators and other prizes.

- Russians drink an average of 4¾ gallons (18 liters) of alcohol per year.

- Russia has over 6375 nuclear weapons. The United States has 5800.

- The USA is often thought of as the main superpower when it comes to nuclear weapons, but the Russian army has the most number of nuclear weapons, about 8400, which is more than any other country in the world.

- In 1961, Yuri Gagarin became the first cosmonaut in space. He made a 108-minute orbital flight in his Vostok 1 spacecraft. In addition to sending the first person into outer space, the Soviet Union also launched the world's first satellite in 1957, known as Sputnik.

- Russia sold Alaska to the United States in 1867 for $7.2 million. Adjusting for inflation, the US bought Alaska for $118 million in today's value.

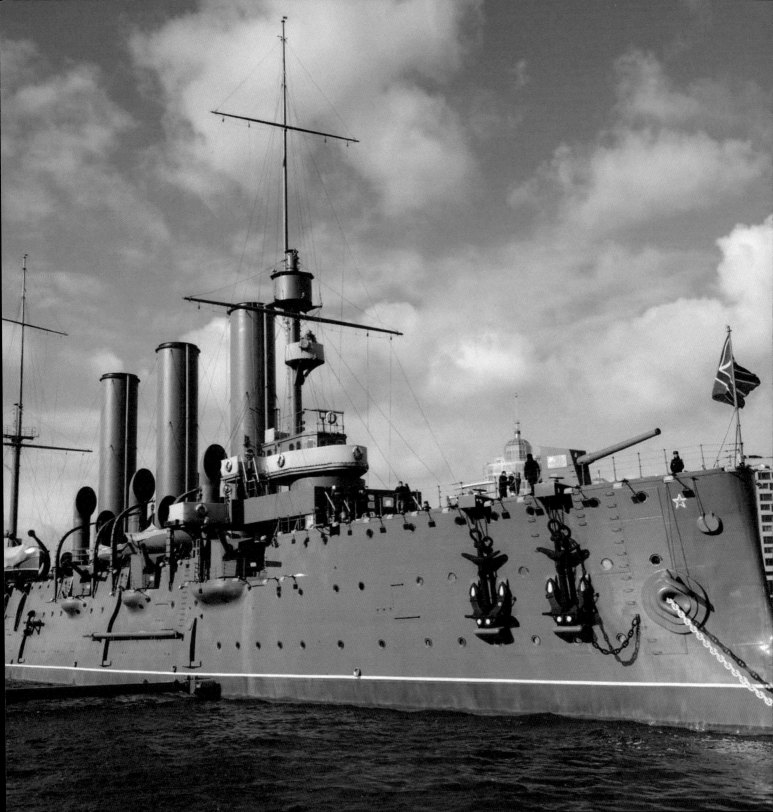

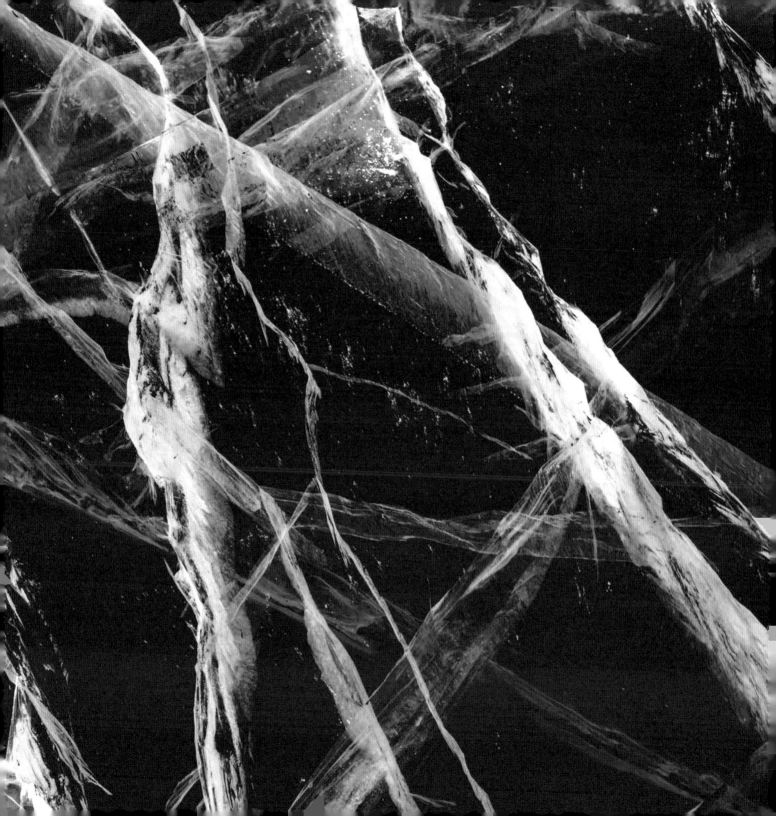